5 Spirits in my Mouth

poems, laments, & incantations

ALSO BY PAN MORIGAN

I, Music Box

Trouble the Waters, Tales of the Deep Blue

(Co-editor & contributor)

5 SPIRITS IN MY MOUTH

poems, laments, & incantations

Pan Morigan

QUERENCIA

Querencia Press, LLC
Chicago, Illinois

CONTENTS

MUSIC STIRRING IN THE GROUND 11

    Strange Midnights 13

    Rootless..15

    Voicings 18

    Open Minor 9..22

    Banjo Lessons..25

    A Simple Song..30

    The Eaten..32

    Eclipsis..33

    The Poems and the Soap 37

CASSANDRA'S LAMENT..41

    Conversations with Cassandras..43

    The Black House..47

    Tiger Tongues..50

    A Woman inside Her Moon..52

    Street Deer 57

    Akhmatova draws a Circle..59

    From the Mouth of the Wounded Dark..63

    Crow-Told..65

    Ancestries..68

DARK STARS BRIGHT WHISPER 72

   Shaking out the Cards 74

   Dark Stars 76

   Amulet 78

   Liminal Round 81

   Whoa Death 86

   Animate 87

   Napalm Head 89

FUGUES & FRACTALS 94

   2 Pi R 96

   Pocketful of Fractals 105

   Lullaby 107

   Alchemy 110

   Five Spirits in my Mouth 111

   Love, Function 118

A SIMPLE SONG 122

   Shakes Her Words 124

FOR AMA

MUSIC STIRRING IN THE GROUND

STRANGE MIDNIGHTS
(FOR SHEREE)

Strange midnights
When a solitary spirit calls
Dressed in a silk suit   slightly frayed

Carrying a banjo
With no strings

Strange midnights

When music pours   from an iron pot
And a voice arises
From one with no mouth

While star-threads lament
And whistle

Strange   strange midnights
Luminous
Disarranged

In squares of moonlight
I tattoo a notebook
With stone and dirt memories

Theories of survival

I imagine you netting blues sonnets
As planets sink into sky-tides
Oh, fisher of beauty

Far   far   away   deep inside   your river
You don't sleep either

We could light candles   lay cards

Instead   we plant seeds in drought
Deliver roots from nightmares

Worrying for loan payments   rent   fire
Open wounds
In the earth of us

Eternity

And the bulb pops!
Expels last lightening

The room goes dark   darker

Strange midnights
Come knocking
Flailing the wild-hewn gourd

Even at this distance
In this   war
A sizzling node connects us

Shimmers
Reignites

Somehow yes and again   yes!
We get to singing!

ROOTLESS

I
Let's yank ear plugs and sit
Where copper plaques commemorate long-dead loves

This patch of city park
With a history

Traffic of the world recedes
Dull undercurrents without nails

Dun helicopter above, twitter-blade
Doesn't even scare the crows, who also thunder

We snatch hands, decline a smoke
Exhale exhaust, consider love

Below us, tough pines and oaks plunge root
Grip mud, suck, suck

Somewhere-under, in dank amphibian dark
Nectar flows, a sweetness we've never known

Asking us to note
The wandering and rooted
The shredded or sleeping

Even the metal beasts
We breathe them

While they breathe us

Feel that?

The whole, messy menagerie
Time and song and fate
Jitterbugging

Footprints of the ineffable
Leading us home

Beneath a black walnut tree

2
Now, rain on parched ground
Hemlocks drink, maples green up

Take what they can get, mix light and will
Leaves unfold and each one is a book

We haven't learned our letters yet

If we study our palms long enough
We may transmute
Hearts, reanimate

While the skies in our bones
Spin gravity

And the salt flats
Of our riverain topologies
Wash away into wilding seas

And our spirits burn
Still knee-deep in honey

3
You say

I don't want to write myownself
Amongst remnant woods, leaking trees

Look

Flies, wrens, foxes, mountains, rivers
Crowds of the humble
Cavort and flip, voiceless

(While humming eternity
Into being)

I say

"Incant, girl
Don't ever stop!"

4
Finally, we receive a message:

Dive for the tangled root
Touch, tune, feel

Learn faster, love harder

Speak multitudes

VOICINGS

In a beginning
vast storms envelop earth
Horses race across broad, dry plains
until, as emptied sacks, they collapse in yellow dust
                         to rise again as whirligigs

From cliffs above, both poet and hunter
observe dual mysteries of time and distance
One, waiting for the kill, expires from thirst
while ghost-steeds tumble
sowing themselves

The other, misunderstanding the meaning of horses
aims flocks of words over bombed-out bridges

Reverberations are heard centuries later
in Chicago trainyards, Dakar subdivisions
along labyrinthian, Istanbul boulevards
through the damaged chambers
of a grocery-clerk's heart

                         All the cities, without, within
               speaking themselves, dreaming in tongues
                    dressing the wind in manifold tones

Do you know this place?
There, words do
Never die

Looping the infinite generations
Singing light-trails, storm-winds, broken moons, concertos

Feather, liver, sigh, scissor, lullaby, map, hand
kidney, oak, mass murder, eye

Woven in withered leaves, trash heaps
Abandoned in gutters
And bombed-out classrooms, echoing

Remembered again, remade
Searching, stuttering, wailing

They have their plan, the little words
Their works, forming universes
which we do spend

And so, upended by prevailing winds
my sonnets become cooked books
Colonial fancies

Art is hung from a branch outside town
Or does the hanging, making orphans

What name, then, for a woman
Who serves all comers
carrying the sick to a stretcher
her hands in life, in death, day and night
yet she never looks away
never flags 'til the shift ends
Then she cries and cries

Somebody stole the word we needed
Sold it to the highest bidder
Was it love, stubbornness, habit
art, ether, science, other?

Even now, a river cuts through intransigent stone
gracious with water-code
giving birth to tributaries, hooks, incantations, odes
And the swift mad horses, last of their kind
stampede until they enter earth again

            leaving a spray of pounded, cracked seeds
            scattered for miles in yellow dunes
                    (a refrain of horses)
                        which become grasses, feeding finches
                                    who trill, causing foxes

    A mouse eats, shits
    Earthworms arrive, revealing many dirty truths
    while the dead horses of language rot
    Then arise, humming

    I water hope in its earthic pot each day
    sow fallow acres with gouts of wordage
    (a preamble to sudden wildflowers I never planted
    genus lost to time, distance, fear, and plunder
    or other silences)

    I think, let my words be clover
    nettle, skin, cyclical, profligate
    May I nourish the ruminants amongst us
    or at least, the remnants—
    before the hunter of meaning returns
    to drain our speakings of blue milk, nectar, and stink

            Let it never be said, there's one beginning only
                or one end

                a single syntax, song, sky, or tongue
                    One way to tell, or spell
                        or address the unspeakable, silent distances

            Silence begs song, yes?
            As death begets dandelions

And I seek the edge of an unknown darkness

since hunter, night, knows other-physics

Seeking some escape hatch, I go a-whirligig
where universes loop one another, ribbonish
and alphabets bloom, extruding universes
Just so, I sing   am sung
simpleminded, furious, fractal-touched, hungering

'til a wild horse, or its ghost, comes stepping
east to west, A to Z
feeds from my hand, leaving me emptied and free
while winds gossip, tuned to the frequency of bees
and blackbirds, cell towers, rivers, freeway traffic, windmills
a street-dweller's ask, an owl's sigh

Yes, even the tall grasses blow and tell
And we emit words, songs
moan, hum, implore, incant, rhyme
in and out of time
and so, believe we exist

If words are wind, rain, amoeba
dirt, struggle, shackle, key
who might we be?
In this moment of terror, be seed
Seed's echo, seed's urge
Be protest and holler, be song
Voicing universes, singing up worlds

A g a I n & again
yes, yes, y   e   s
I r & u 2

B, 2

Sung-b
ThIs woR(l)d
syn

chroni c   i   t   y

OPEN MINOR 9

Another dark afternoon, cloud-draped
Fog-lit, with cantankerous sun-hiccups
Rain tantrums turn to snow mess on my roof

Wind throws fits

Nobody can decide who to be
Or how, or when, or why
And my friend arrives just in time

(Sky-blue shirt, beat-up guitar)

He's excited—has discovered a sound
Pulls up a chair, face lit from within
Strums

An open minor 9 bounces off the walls and floor

I found this chord!

Like an ancient wayfarer
Plumbing tectonic notions in a rented dream
Of a vintage pub under blue-green water
On the far side of twilight

He hollers, *I'm so inspired!*

And I can't say it
I mean, why would I? So I don't
(An open minor 9 ain't news, guys!)

Still, we jam on
Singing like marionette ships

Bouncing with a goofy frisson

Two planets from wobbling universes
Sharing rivers

We're like a posy growing upside-down
In the palm of a leather girl
Buried in a frozen bog

She expired in a field of purple heather
One long-ago, spring
Humming proto-mother goose

When even wolves were wet behind the ears

And ta-da!
Here we are!
Braiding our ghosts to symphonic rains
The sound of right now

Drumming up a cure for melancholia
All the existential horrors

Aching with poignant mysteries
Bursting to be told

And memories
Of things we've never done

Yeah, we reinvented the wheel
Remembered how to be alive for once
Leaping into waterfalls of song

Like the first note ringing out
At the beginning of all rhythm and rhyme

(Cause each mote of life is newly born
a zillion times
In the hand that loves enough
To feel, sense,
Groove and
howl...)

Ah, the scent of spaghetti and onions on a stormy afternoon!

You place the guitar on the floor
With tender ceremony
Pour wine, nod, guffaw

It's nothing big you know, yet somehow
Every bitty thing

Yeah, *everything*
That could ever be
Or become
Has transpired in one half hour
Of laughing
And thrumming

Nothing much
But *all*, right?

A tasty sip of music
An open, minor 9

BANJO LESSONS

The banjo makes me sing
Gourd-child
Of the N'goni, the Akonting

Mali hums through a buzzing ring
Bambara bounce, Wolof mouth, and a Senegal port
Jola fingerprints don't wash out
Raleigh-stains bruise a tightened skin
New Orleans floodtides rise up the neck

Jim Crow stole it
Busted levees drowned it
And my painted mouth hides
No minstrel truth

Hear Appalachian ballads come tumbling
New England ring shout: sacred discredited
Decca records pays a penny a recording, then you're done
Cake Walk!

Fox trot orchestras, up to the knees in it
The riot and the lynch of it
Medicine show, and a jamboree
Forked tongue twang

Stealth genius stokes rebellion
All-Black radio percolating innovation
Connecting constellations and multiple moons
To liberation

Pouring musical libation
From Memphis to New York
Montgomery to Chicago

And all the nameless hamlets in between

Race records

Yeah, everybody tries to claim or shame a banjo

At the airport
Mr. Georgia-Tech gives me a nod
"Go South!"
Banjo passport
To amnesiac nostalgia?
(Because, these freckles?)

As if Americana was ever a whites-only jam

Meanwhile some look askance at a country thang
So embarrassing
Or laugh
Hey, seen that movie, Deliverance?

Folk dramas play on...
But who gets delivered?
Nobody knows what they're really saying

Except the banjar

Bringing a primal whine
A night-schooled wail
Some pay-check lender's Hail Mary

Revealing our gun-toting
cross-burning American secrets
Supposed to stay hidden
Behind that skin... but won't

As if you could stuff history in the back of a bus
Send it circling the prison yard

Felon for life, hijacked rights
Lost at the last polling station, shut tight, early

As if history and all her blessed children
Would not get up before dawn
Bus in, demand a say. Again. Again

And now this lightening rod burns my wrists
Haunted so deep, it gives me the creeps
Zombie tones, truth jones

Cold hands walk up my neck as I sing
Snuff-tales trussed up in that metal ring
Ill at ease, suffering, denying, lying

So blue, the appropriation-riff

Andrew Jackson and his lunatic legacy
Mr. Slaver-Ethnic-Cleansing, all scrubbed up
For that new, Texan, anti-history book

(Or was it Florida?)
Still filthy

Defied the supreme court, made sport
Of murdering Black Folks
Seminoles, Creeks, Cherokees...

He wasn't alone
No rogue out there on his own
Black towns in Iowa, we burned to the ground

Oklahoma, Kansas, Florida, too
East St. Louis massacre
And somewhere near me and you

A trail of ebony tears, denied

See the rime of salt and ash on the E string or the A?
Banjar's metal pot will shriek, wake you, nights
Those frets shall cut, bleed you

Banjar sings, wails in tongues

You dream Rhode Island death ships
Carolina slavers
Boneyards, rail yards, stockyards, prison yards
Mineshafts stuffed with buried evidence

All the way to this very day

And the banjo keeps insinuating
Inciting, indicting
Laying a hoodoo spell

Pounding *us* into my throat
Wang dang doodle and the contradictions sing!
So impolite, so messed up

So right

This land is your land
And we shall overcome
(Bless ol' Pete and Fannie Lou)

Mojo modes roll on
Troubling the waters from Benin to Sapelo
Cape Fear to the Chesapeake

Jordon river rising

C'mon, move your feet
Grab a stranger by the hand
I'll try if you cry out

We'll sing and tell, frail and rant
Get back that voting rights act

'Cause nobody can stop this keening song
This angry, laughing tongue

Truth, ringing out in code—I'm listening

Won't hide from history
Wear it, choke on it
The bloody and the ugly

Complicity, sealed in the middle of this skin
Can't make what was, all right
Not with a banjo!

Something so all-America
Here in my arms, singing so strong
So beautiful, bleak, and fierce
Oh, so wrong

But I carry it, right?
Goddamn you, America
I'm gonna carry it
For *love*

We gotta carry it!

Carry

It

All

A Simple Song

Late sun in November
Molten elements twist

Light falls fast

We race frost-tipped leaves
skirt the owl's house
(Up a headstrong oak
back of the package store)

Falling into one another
Grasping motes of laughter
We're our own bonfire, make-fare
Until spring emits another appearance

In cold-maker streets
We count on that rhythm
Dandelions bursting in a bitsy grass-patch
Bees tapping the windowpane

Making hope from pollen
And song
Or from nothing at all

This, our stubborn call
We shout it over hard-lit plains
The rubbled city

For now, blackbirds snatch last threads of light
The sun paints herself, drunk

Meteors scrape messages above
We can't read them
But we feel the score

A round for sixteen thousand spirits
Shaker and a tag-sale violin

The train-yard crickets chant
Navigating shadow
Memory is their power

We breath them and they, us
Together for one more round

Autumn spills blue light from her rusted pail
Then the longer walk

Our troubles scattered 'cross the ground
Almost there

Almost there

We know the route
By sorrow and leaf
Work
Music

And deep inside our dogged dreaming
Friend dusk

Comes singing
Singing
Singing

THE EATEN

5 minutes to save yourself
and the bitchy neighbor (if time is real)
5 minutes to grab the fiddle, snatch the wheel
turn off the gas, light first fires
5 minutes to a brass ticket
unholy grail
mad dash
last chance, vote
apologize to your lover
you're home
hair on fire
equally, a runaway
lost in the slipstream
5 minutes to rewrite all words
every aching failure
to learn the first note of the first song
again and again, for always
every *impossible* notwithstanding
just as a tempest improvises
last seas—our chains
and hollow claims turn to breeze, pollen
we're lost in the puff, fluff
the wonder, singing along
in five minutes
we are swan
we are heron
kissing night's lip, laughing
embracing all the crosswinds
moon-cycles, time-fumbles
drinking the darkness
so good

oh, so good!

ECLIPSIS

1

A thousand years past in spring
a poet climbed mountain cliffs
At the summit, remote as clouds
a blackbird lay, stone bitten

She, the poet, took from her pack a lump of ink
mixing it with water from the creek
Also at hand, a horse-hair brush
paper of fiber and leaf
white skies on which to remake, redo

With instruments arrayed in hope
she penned a simple query
Why had time not waited for those she loved
to finish their long, hard bloom?

Why had time not waited?

2

Early winter, leaving work

I enter haunted evening
Sleet sings itself to earth
I doubt I can finish life's tasks in time
Yet I've earned no rights to despair

Tracking cloud calligraphy across a dim horizon
I await the late train

Shredding newspapers marred by ink scars
I ask the emptied station
we'll arise in love, won't we?

A you-shaped hole wavers, nodding
opposite the platform
Awaiting transport
from another dimension

My train goes one-way too
a sweeping arc
Invading neighborhoods of soot-brick
Windows close enough to touch

Wash is left on the line for a season
Shirts, socks, faded dresses, frozen stiff
Abandoned promises rattle the stars
Porch furniture tipped over, clangs the wind, unheard

Yellow kitchen lights burn all hours for years

A tattooed man steps onto a fire escape
hunches over rusted railings
lights his match in the gathering squall
I think, farewell strange ship

Have you done what you meant to?

My thoughts leap chasms of space-time, stuttering
I hear you inside me
your voice a silvered stream
that won't stop ringing

(Snow piles to Mars,
wind shreds skin)

Never will I see you again

Are all travelers so bereft of shelter?
no way to splint stone-bitten wings?

Is our shared moment a speeding train, late again?
a ghost nodding off, always waiting?

Maybe only severed feathers dance

Only lost dreams sing, ascending remote cliffs
Daring the ice that rings in us
to give way
Become warm rain

At last, the night-train shakes distant tracks

Your voice echoes
We get on, we get off, we come, and we go
It's an elliptical world

Will you return to me at dawn
riding your ghost-pain?

Might I track some wanderer's steps
Become mist-riddled cliff
Tattooed blackbird?

Is there no difference
between poet and mountain

Cloud
and crumpled newspaper

Each of us awaiting the fate that erases all distance?

Will my questions go unanswered
thousands of years?

Do we learn a mourning heart each time

all by ourselves

      Alone, alone?

As if that song were new as first light

                  or last

                        Never before
                            heard

    or

          sung?

The Poems and the Soap

Possible!
To make from night a handful of clay
With that, to shape idols of our sorrows

Broken faces
Rent innards
Bent symphonies

We bow to them as blue stars protest

Possible!
To sear hope in an iron pot, white hot
Scatter cinders across a path to dreams
Or to soup, at least

Until we're parched and lost, but fed
(A handful of yellow petals to our names
And summer laughing, *you liars!*)

Possible!
To set adrift the ships of grief and dread
Throw wide each rusted door
Revealing a fortress of heartbreak
Immovable as buried skies

Possible, just about

Though our day off
Is one short, sweaty, hell of worry

Yelling at senators about voting rights
Choking on the tangled root
Twelve errands meaningless

Histories clamouring to be known
The poem never written
Dead battery, lost key, last dollar

All the way 'round to midnight
That cold clay

Nevertheless, what shall we make?
'Cause I heard a stone speak
Declaring its own tongue

The grasses danced their knives and swords
Among willows bordering the dump

An owl sang
Possible! Possible!

We went to do laundry
It was hot

We slumped in bony chairs
Minds spinning with the dryers

A ladybug landed on the windowsill
Threw wide her dotted dress
Daring summer wilds

I no longer need the flame
Wanna borrow it a while?

Possible, you blurted
To sing a broken sky!
Another lost afternoon—that music

Fevers, buried dreams, five years gone untold

Chant the washer and the broom too, I said
The poems and the soap
A wrench, some nails, or rusted screws

Attaching life to itself

All the unfinished things
Scarred by hope

(Moon-willows whispering
A lump of clay, a spade
Cello, flute, violin
Your voice seeking home)

Yeah, all the little things
And bits of time

And dirt
And love
And breath

Each singing their days
And byways

Telling their times
And tragic ends

Making possible
From nothing much at all
Or even less!

So why not you and I, friend?"

CASSANDRA'S LAMENT

CONVERSATIONS WITH CASSANDRAS
(FOR LIZ)

Alone at midnight, I wonder what is real

In some vast desert or rubble city
Leopard-selves hack endangered laughter

How can I ask?

Lost geese and shepherds of histories
Toil over impassible mountains, gulping colonial frequencies
A thousand unjust acts upend worlds, in shouting distance

Hearts are rent and no bell tolls
I ask!

O sing a song of realizms trampling the wild grasses of
unknowing & vanity pickup trucks draped in rags of manifest
cruelty & poisoned lipsticks corroding her outlawed mouth &
brain-chips taking selfies at Virus Warehouse & freedom-lies
cocked to pop off & blues-leaf-litigants pounding pavements
expiring for lack of falsifiable arguments, etc., etc., etc.

To whom, (it may concern you) I wail discredited grooves
rebellious for connection (Committing poetry-crimes by the
dozen) But my damned device finishes every sentence

Abracadabra
            Tame as beige air
                        I'm rendered *Standard Anglais*

Relatabull

                        Yet

something ineffable
shouts, hey, hey, wait!
The elemental
bursts, laughing

Fractals
weep
and
alphabets
atrophy

fragile as butterflies in amber

Whole languages
epic songs
are gutted
on a disembodied platter
And my art fails to save the world

Again

Grasping the uncharted notebook
I ask

Which remedy can I offer, sing, rant?
What changes because of my attention?

Pound passion
Say kind bricks and rafters, apparently listening
Let tendons speak
Say pencils and chatty sheets of paper

Real as pain you are
Real as hell on earth

Why, you're solid as machine-gun fire
Buckshot spray and stolen days
A feather exchanged for a life

You're serious as the daily grind
Real as easy slanders cloning themselves
Legalized larceny
Another Jim Crow'd vote

You ask the wrong questions!

Taste thought, says blue ink
Become unthinkable
Seed history in your melody, says fiddle
Be transgressive and slippery

Hear pine's needle too, says the Tupelo tree
And the mourning streets in the root of your belly
(The ink chimes in again)
Taste, touch, dance, feel, make stuff!

Feel everybody
Everybody's pain

Find a realm in torn pockets or in your left eye
Hand it off to some wayfaring stranger

Question your questions
Shred the edges of your narratives
Take note of our monstrous ancestors

'Cause bodies await your bone-book, grief-bound
Your stone-thoughts, straight-up, no chaser
Your honeycomb physics, revelatory quakes

The clay of murdered story, reanimate

Somebody says and means it
Share tears, spirit fissures, heart rubble
Make some noise!

Bang your cracked vessel with bent, analog spoons
If the kitchen goes up in flames
Play your rhythms on earth's palm

Love somebody else's dream how you love your own!

And when life hurts like hell
Speak, sweat, and tell
Like you got skin in the game

And yes, the night heaves, breaks
Yes, yes, comes another day

The sea forms stars
From jewel foam and merciless reflections

While we, shackled to rivers of distraction (Curated
by vampires—mountaintop-removal of the mind)
Sleep on through the many silencings

Losing count of cut-down, cut-up lives

Dear poet, singer, maker, we're shite out of time!
Hear that song so surrealistically real?

The Cassandras are prophesizing
Like screaming, bleeding birds

Life herself is testifying
Begging
To be heard

THE BLACK HOUSE
(COOKING WITH FRIENDS, DISCUSSING
JEB BUSH'S 2016 CAMPAIGN SPEECH)

Let's cook

Mixing spice and thought
As good chefs ought

Treasures of cinnamon

Hot pepper, garlic and ginger
Plus history
Joined in a mortar

Of memory

Let's stir up a thousand acts
Lies and buried facts
Greasy sunsets in a bag of black-eyed peas

A stew of mighty Atlantic storms
Stolen recipes
Igbo rice and garlic shrimp

Amnesia

Final suppers
Sunken ships
Bloodied spread sheets

Bambara lullabies
Shaking Savannah oak leaves
Down gracious redbrick, mansion-streets

Ornamented in Yoruba black-smithery

The sly investments of bankers and their wives
Whose children run for president

(Only their names appear
on commemorative plaques)

Ah, the scent of baked-in legacies

Let's sing a song of the children of presidents
Who also run for president

Today, we'll mix spices
For a fiery American pot
As one of those, in the news
Blathers 'bout *no free stuff for Blacks*

Helluva nerve
Black America, unpaid
Ploughed your fields, hundreds of years
Raised your barns and your babies, too

While, innovating
And inventing
Transforming
This entire world

Our country, tis of thee
(Fifty states
and the territories)
Owes a mighty mess of Black back-wages

Yet here you sit, pontificating...
Fingers in the pot
Awaiting coronation
Assume it a rich, white guy's given

Call our Jim Crow hegemony
Your burden

(While through some clever sleight of hand
still don't know who made your ass)

No, you don't know our story
I mean all of us

America

'Cause nobody is talking
Some commodity-crap free stuff, man
We owe a country
An entire Black land

A pile-up of centuries to every Black hand

40 acres, health insurance
Jazz *and* the hoppin' john

Black legacy
Burning your mouth
Feeding your bank account
North and south

Yes, we'd best start calling it
The Black House

Now, cooking finished, our dish is served

Taste, Mr. Prez-in-waiting
Enjoy

And pay the bill
Like a gentleman

Tiger Tongues

When twilight folds over day
and the river stops

I listen at the little things of life
stirring around me and within

The rug, thin, endures my step
Swept clean
the floor groans

Radiators sing to air

Unhurried   a wolf appears
at the screen door
searching for the source of all water

A green heron bursts from the sky of our walls
bringing inner rain
and no maps

Tigers slap slivers of sun off a three-legged table
While hawks arc over black thunderheads
on the ceiling

I regard my scribble   the fallow acres
Breathe the fractured moment

How swiftly a mad whirligig changes our town
an entire land
even a raptor's heart!

Where will we be when lightning strikes twice?
Will the gates hold   or the doors?

Which ghosts will accompany us
down roads of manufactured chaos?

What difference   between my workaday trudge
and a poem or song
Scribbled on the back of the gas bill?

Will I notice when something eternal breaks
disintegrating
with a silent call
or hiccup?

Will I exclaim   how we sang!
How we've been sung!

Or will the tigers return
disguised as shadow?

Slipping through
the membranes of our disbelief

As the many little things of life are swept into a sea of night

into black rivers

thick with stars

Upended

A WOMAN INSIDE HER MOON

1

Six nights of intimate moon, my loves   Snow, electric white
on a cunning branch   Slow whispers off black mica roofs   Icicle
light and moon bane on knife sky   A dark blade takes breath
Slicing the flesh of her awareness   Slivers of I
fly reform shatter   Ripe and wet and meat, the orb of being
fading, halving, calving, and reforming   The world divides
moans, reunites   Freezing grasses clump up and cling
to themselves   A million sovereign slivers or tunes make their
rhythms known to unknown places

Rabbit footprint runs, jumps without form across darkness
Shadows, we too, myself and you, search for selves of bark or leaf
steel, skin, synapse-screw, and mythological fur   Needing song
to pass along, hand to hand, down millennia of forgotten sacks
erupting from brazen, frost-bitten skin   We make a stand
of willow sewn with yellow roots and schools of carp, catching
each-and-other's attention in nets of sighs, battling highest
altitude   Flocks of hot-green ducks and milky spores raft rivers
Lapping the heels of under-things seeking paths through dunder-
brush and femicide

2

Old fat moon wraps self around fugue clouds
Smiles, knowing her refrain can never be unsung, unmade
Says, drop your burdens and the weight of story-stones
The wounds, infection, damage, wrecked histories, tattoos
The cicatrix   Other holy indicators
Take stock of ruinous calculations
Search out remedies for a fiery electric madness
that comes of living under-boot
Our jets of sentient blood reaching through hell, to starlight

3

Say now...
deer leap, rabbit tell, horn head speak!
She invents or dies
Her scrawl, a rusted, half-told tale, pumps rough
skips beats, gasps disbelief
Without your looking, you believe she's mist   meat
So go your way   and I'll offer my agreements to ghosts
To ant owl, elephant, rattlesnake, bee   We become
Shifting, making, undoing, reforming, remembering

I agree with goosewing, cow-pat, crow-talk, river-smack
With tree rebellions and the revolutions
of muck-divers, thunder scatterers, and invisible people
I repeat and incant impossible equations
while feting pissed-off noisy women   I want to hear from them
Wander kidnapped landscapes   painted, carved, filmic
Gasping for air, breathing in, out   Singing songs and laments
of stolen serving-girls turned into vases

Yet, this prison of taxonomies isn't airy enough
for those of crushed stone   however grandiloquent
or noble the essentialism   I refute the words you claim and
maim me with   How you measured, catalogued, undid!
Loved, reviled, bought, stole, mined, and drained!
You did so, but you're not the overlord of my narrative
I slice through your ball of yarn and float unmoored, straining
for any moon—fleshly or grammatical   Chasing our blood
off your maps and charts, flying past eminent delusions
self-replicating, statistical conclusions, deadly algorithms
You and your infectious rashes of surreptitious-plundering-
surveillance-imagery-humiliation-museum dogma
and demonizing, bully gods

You know who *you* are
With that ever-replicating, viral impunity

While I, I have become an explorer

Finding your *realizms* spurious and weighty beyond measure
Retro, twice-gravity, and so very boring   I will be an astronaut
clawing wind, a sea-diver clinging to no tide   Pouring over cliffs
of word-traps to another side   I'm the sea and the multitude
of earths asking, not as thought experiment, but straight up
as blunt accusation   How many womanish ones have you
dismembered, de-animated in your particular profession?

It occurred to me today as I considered the grinding silence
imposed on my spirit, that most stories, songs, movies, epics
myths, corporations, spread sheets, and closely held beliefs would
not exist if the inventor-author-maker hadn't slandered
or erased, raped, mutilated, gagged, burnt, murdered some female
in the first frame, scene, chapter, and verse   Imagine how
creation arrives with our blood, gushing unsung   How many
epic tales or sales would sputter to an end before attaining
their eminently rotting fruition without that slit, blood-slicked
corpse-us

Like life and not
A fairy tale, movie, entertainment, empire, holy dogma, psalm
poem, song, law

Like so many surviving this carnival of empire, I'm an escapee
slinging defiance at silence, at any body rendered regulatory site
I've amassed enough escape to scrawl moon-words
across wind, though none may hear   (Don't assume
since I've mentioned moon + gender + silence
that you can snare this rabbit)   What has moon-ranting to do
with cosmological agreements or disagreements for that matter
Or with the fact that I write of spaceships, talking animals
the mutability of my mind in one torn sentence

And wear diving gear even while sleeping

I'll leave you to consider on your own time
the speculative nature of a woman's existence
Her zillion attempts at flight   Her edifices of bones, hawk-
feathers, wooden spoons, buckets, placentas, bloody rags and
brooms, beads, crocheted harts, conquests, crowns, cycles and
scars, flagrant hats, weapons   Her taints and chains of disguise
The obligatory elastics, cookie cutters, still births, re-formed
flesh, fishing nets, acres of invention, and hopeless ecocide
I need another mood so I walk on my hands, toes, head, or
undulate across the floor 'til I get there   I want another way
of singing   A new way to dance my forgotten physics, strut my
charred incantations   I won't care if my verbiage doesn't suit or
if I'm ugly-angry-known.   I've sworn to the knife of night I'd
step out, in, and across this milky way flying palace
Alone or with you

4
C'mon hear my dead-of-night-scrawl
Thunder is my ride
Medusa and her hideous sisters, I claim and adore
The skinning knife I keep at my side—inside my boot
Aiming high (low) or wherever most appropriate
I might have been dead stones or burned faggots like many
I dodged and ducked   Learned to read   Rewrote the rote

Now I begin again in silence or noisiness to learn what comes
of tangled midnight, when many sleep but forget to dream
I wake as old moon starts her hour of gossip and taletelling
My hands, callused, stubborn, seek the roots of words
I listen for inner-dictionaries, sentences that don't exist   She is
talking at me and we agree, me and Moon   She's like me
I know by the marks of land-rovers and space-grubbers
across her back and belly   The digital maps of her crevasses
and valleys, hurts and wonders   Her light-born languages
of subterfuge and fantastical liberations, ill-considered alliances
The betrayals, compromised positions, plundered, discredited
histories   The footprints on her face and the flag up-plunged into
her heart, among other exploding ordinance

Moon is measuring out her long hidden grief
Asking me to tell how it feels to be eaten
No matter the hopeful agreements made
or language upended—

Feel: slandered, rent, in pieces, de-animate
Feel: dysmorphia'd, never heard from, or seen

And the many burials
The many burials
The ones never found or freed

And us wrestling the thousand forms of gravity—
telling the same story again

Being halved, calved, frayed, slandered, reclaimed
forgotten, sold, reborn, erased, again, again, again

Lifting this rock of ache
from earth to sky to sea to hell
over and over

As if womanish ones had nothing else to do or be
Or to become

No other races to run

Do you copy, Houston?

STREET DEER

I'm scared every day, have I said?
Thought there was another mirror
Under the lake
On the clouds
Surely one day there would be escape
A path across prairie grasses
Veils of art to hide behind
And run, run forever
Refuge of a sort
While my spirit gestated
And I unburied my nest
Building it at the same time
On the horizon
From threads of star and darkness
Until I became a song
Brave lava, leaping fire
Crumbled statuary
Signaling other worlds
That I dreamed in symphonic fugues
And panic overtaking the days
Always running
Never far enough
From horned beasts, prowling
Their packs of cold-eyed followers
Crowned with ever-indelible impunity
Bellowing poison smoke at new worlds
Limbs flung wide
Across the seats, the streets
Turf-marking each alley, plaza, country
Culling me again and again
In the night
On my dime
Until nightmares rode me
Dream and desire atrophied

When they burned my mouth
Twelve times over
And I was charred from within
Silent
When they emptied my tongue
Of its plan
Of its place
Its origin-moon-chase and vast plain
When my head was disabused of a proud tilt
My neck, bent
My spirit-dress, deemed a dirty failure
Running circles of derision
Spinning until I curled
Burnt leaf, wrung out
Used, recalibrated
Smiling the damn smile
Quick tail
Furred face
Crooked hoof
Scarring self
Craven-pleasing
'Til our will is replaced
Rage disguised
Without scent
Or trace

So hopefully

There's no more reason
To kill us

Akhmatova draws a Circle

luminous
her musing in a black and white photograph

illusive
the mood emanating from paper skin
lips pressed firm and soft   to swallow
murmur

her raw tongue
darning words
igniting verbs rolled in ash

a narrow window is framed in soot-blackened angels
doves peck bloody crumbs off the marble sill

the poet glances left, eyes of blue-black glass, heavy-lidded
revealing the unspeakable

seventeen months waiting
with throngs of the hollow-cheeked

stolen weeks of winter
pawing prison walls

hoping for glimpses of companions
a cousin, the child

survival, some trick in war-battered St. Petersburg

entire Romany orchestras board trains to oblivion
last songs are squeezed from brown violins

a long-dead friend sips tea
brings news of another denunciation

first the synagogue, painted yellow
then the theater, burnt

now fragile sun slants though refugee birch groves
alabaster roots   twist   and ache
a wash of rainbow hues shattering

the poet gathers sorrows   knits silence
relics of memory

refining a calligraphy of endurance
weight become light

observing without flinching
barbed wire horizons
typhoid winters

friends   artists   lovers   singers and scientists
rendered complicit   or conscripted   exiled

lost songs
left to sing themselves
lard smoking in a stewpot
a kitchen of clamor and rubble
the poet's son, ill in the cells
rendered bargaining chip

she penned a half-cocked screed for the dictator
with that pistol to her head

who wouldn't?

government tools proclaimed her whore, a danger
her poems, woman's pestilence
compromised

covered in insult
her artistry remained inviolate

she said
my task is to keep free this tongue
of multitudes

alone she stood, and stood
carving verses from winter stones
a massif of ghosts

rising in mists at midnight
for millions buried nameless
in ice-bound gulags

she wrote and wrote

and on her heels
generations of upstart girls
tongues unfree

scratch for sun
with paint and ink on journal pages
joining impossible fights
with vindictive oligarchs

trembling through kill-nights
stitching scraps of battered light
drawn on raw-tongue flesh

banging electric guitars with wounded fingers
from Moscow to Kyiv
down ash streets unmade
Damascus, Yangon, Flint, L.A.

they don't give up

let them not give up

Akhmatova
or her spirit
her memory
puts down the leaking pen
gazes out history's window
sips tea

asking
who is beast
and who, man?

tearing from mind and heart
Words
Words

offering them as amulets
for her time

and every-every place

this frozen earth
with poems
she fed

and us girls
finally

we also
ate

FROM THE MOUTH OF THE WOUNDED DARK

First:
Rain falls in bricks
Trees shudder, bracing themselves
Our roof leaks in five places

A river rises and earth cracks, exposing the future
Looks like drunk oil-tankers, roller-skating

Second:
Rabbits startle, leap to ground
Hearts rattle, tiny hammers denting the jewelry of life
(Gold dust fevers, copper run-off swallowing tongues)

Grey foxes slip into the shed and scream
Fearing the thunder of us
How we make messes

Thirdly:
We get busy, scratching our names on the moon
Extracting riches from mole hills
Eating mountains
Singing like a god

At the four-count:
We flee, enter living caves
Beside the wide Missouri

This Otoe place
Jiwere place

(A cottonwood quivers at our step
Though we fancy ourselves respectful)

Stone birds soar

Ten-thousand-year-old dancers
Keep their own time

Antelopes graze
The limestone rockface

Tamara wuz her, 1977
Luvd u till the ends of time

& Earl turned ten
Again and again

Lastly:
From the mouth of the wounded dark
A refrain

Wear night skin-close
'til rocks burn
And rivers flood

Stirring up your names

Carve tomorrows
From limestone hurts

Remembering
What life is to itself

And, what we've been
To her

CROW-TOLD

Dawn strings skeins of pearl across brown grasses
Swaying neither east nor west
Limp in still air

Coal ash clogs the mouth of the hurricane

Everybody keeps talkin' how dark winter has been
Day after day of gray-relentless

We don't mention the jet stream, that primordial current
Flat-lined across the plains

Nothing doing, nothing moving, heavy as fate
The rains hidden away

Makes the heart shudder
The singers, falter

Their millennia-old stream of song, guttered
Interrupted

Still, gray dew kisses my fingers
As I count stones, bits of blue glass, and backyard clutter

Treasure for a crow-fellow dressed in disheveled feathers
Like some passionate nightclub singer

And the curious eye
Available to intra-species encounters
(Friendship! Spaceship!)

Brightening our heavy-dark meanings at dawn

Together, we look for a rhythm
Some transformative dance step

A call to stir the zombie air
Free our cornered dreams

I find myself wondering
If 5G Minotaurs are squatting in the bandwidth
Allotted to ancestors
Artists, dreamers
Phantoms

A final conquest of liminal space?

Is that why the connective tissue
Between wind, grass
And song is frayed?

Stuck things create unbearable heat
Captive energy smoldering

Dammed blood boils over
Explodes

An electro-emotional field is pinned to the walls
The wind freezes, mid-scream
Carbonized

Meanwhile, the mystery of it all, apparently
Is a heap of beans
Or bones
Ditto history

Our imaginations fail
Crooked rows of thirsting grasses
Unsung

Crow says
Bring your water thoughts

Body-knowledge
Fields of feeling
Your best yelling

And a little respect when you come home

So I say a little prayer for the jet stream
The ghosts of art, science, music, hope

And we keep singing

Even in the dark, the drought
The trembling

Crow and I, together
Flipping chips of blue glass
Like feverish gamblers

Amassing heaps and troves
Of ephemeral shimmer

Wishful

Millennial stones

ANCESTRIES

Always another island
Another meadow, city, continent
Wandering river, stream, wine sea
More swamps, valleys, deserts, hills, arroyos
Piles of rocks, bones, middens of thingies
You chart, map, un-name
Even bluebirds and their hidden routes to water
Inscribed for a billion years on flashing indigo synapses
Always, the willows or the robin's nest
Red-winged blackbird, shy fox, lady's slipper blowing
Spin-up spider, baobab, birch, saguaro, cedar
Trout or whale flipping over white caps, you tally
And the inland lakes, one, two, four and more, to plunder
All things, all beings, all waters, all blood, all speakings
You render inanimate, meat
Inert, a heap, this primordial stone
You've looted each corner of the finite garden
With an acquisitive hand
Conjured scapegoats as cover
Manufactured poverty
Blamed the hungry
And now the horizon wraps around itself
I meet you where I left you
Feeding warrior fires, claiming turf
Your heart is a cauldron of heavy metals, a battlefield
Rocks melt, seas burn
A child scrapes strings and sings
Her voice, buried deep in storm
All that was, becomes its opposite
The wheel stops spinning, but you can't get off it
Splintered seasons become a rack and you, ruin
Wounds of history fester
Once you were seasoned with sacred rimes
Winter your skin-bone

Spring your blood-song
Your shelter, the greenwood, the silver grove
Falling seeds to summer, a gift you did not recognize
You *forgot* as your fathers before you
Replacing the book of the eternal leaf
With visions of apocalypse
Told in holy volumes—fairy tales made truth
Through generations of repetition, then raw deed
Despite your fervent prayers
You became a disease vector, plague dealer
Inventing *bad bodies* to struggle in your slander-scripts
Your tongue, a shredded treaty
Disappearing ink on skin of ash
A false signature
You wrote your tale in hurt, becoming what you made
Dragged us through your mythology
The offspring, the tools, and fools of us
The spears of a nation
Sucking xenophobias
All of us—branded with your make
Likewise, those who never, ever called your name
Or chose your game or agreed to play
Yet they pay and pay
Put dirt in your pocket and flee
The only road was the one you burnt
Run home and cry for your children
They've caught the fever
And you are fear's own face
Brethren? Sisters? Those you ate
Is it for me to repeat the words
You taught me to hate?
To become you, speak death
Take, take, take?
Desperate, I arouse a fractured tongue
Scrawl words in sovereign dirt
Tattoo boundaries of rebellion

On maps of crying lands
Scratching furrows to un-plow
The contested acre of my flesh
Feeding tattered shoots
Fragile veins of raw ideas, half-formed, wet
I, plunderer's seed, refuse your legacy
Showing by this quartered, orphaned heart
I mean it

"Nah" you say, shoving me again
To the front of the breadline
The edge of the cliff

"Come, feast on pain and contraband
The stolen roots

I've transformed worlds to fodder
All for you"

But I know what I feel and see
Reject the monstrous alchemy
Refuse your berserker imaginings

I struggle for some spirit-trace
A reckoning

By sky and water
Flesh and song

I'll find
Some other way
To be

DARK STARS
BRIGHT WHISPER

SHAKING OUT THE CARDS

Tossing shells and rusted coins
Face to a folded sky
Seeking signs of rising sap
Some way to carry on

(A reel for the end, at least
A jig for the rewind)

The hanged man only smiles

See the fingered coppers shimmer
Seasons fumble into place
(Ah, the broken spokes and roots unmade)
And look, the snake, the snake!

Oh, hawk tail brush me now
Queen of hearts tell
If I knew the song before I sang
Wouldn't need this wishing well

And I'd cry no more

I'm wet as saplings in a marsh
Despite this pile-up of years
Bending to insistent winds
Changing shape in every storm

Step back, fate, and you too, chance
I'll do my time 'til the wheel squeals
Pounding a cracked and brazen tune
Searching for a tough refrain

Inside-out, right-side down
Tangled up, all undone

(Damn this grief, this slap-stick world
Making and unmaking

Every, little, lonesome thing
Taking, taking, taking)

See the wild shadows loom
Of all the unlived days

The things I meant to fix, or say
(And other rope and other plays)

Shall I hang myself with hope again?

Dusk replies...
Crashing hard
Then harder

I burn the cards!

Night slips in, soft and damp
Fragrant, plump
Unfolds her ashen petals

Something stubborn
Reawakes, lifts its snout
Bursts into blossom

Tries again
And again

I take a breath
Have a laugh
Still more than glad
To stick around

Dark Stars Bright Whisper

To undo time
Slip inside time
Breath by breath

Swim hard
Each season
Of work, longing
And bone

To have time
Be had

Until sundown
Softens
The clamor of our chaos

Leaving behind
A shared pulse
Skin weaving skin
Within the honey-comb

To keep time
Dance
Out of time

Bumbling through
Mischievous dreams
And midnight's
Untold
Stories

Our rowdy dance, upended

To transcend
These mean ol' times

Feel
Moon's rhythm
In every wounded throat

Renewing our tides, orbits
And holy shadows
Again
Again

Us, all
Learning
The ways we begin
And end
And begin

Struck by awe
Lost to self

Found once more
In the vast, timeless dark

Sensing
Feeling
How stars bright-whisper

On and on

From beyond
Their own
Bright
Deaths

AMULET

(AFTER A PAINTING BY REMEDIOS VARO
TITLED *MÚSICA SOLAR*.)

A woman dressed in fur and flower, periwinkle skin
Plays a single sunbeam with her horsehair bow

This spectral sound, more hue than tune
From an instrument unknown
Never heard by ears alone
Helps the willow, oak, and hemlock overcome

New leaves press through tangled wounds
Under blistering skies ringed by fire
Forming a haven for claw things
And raptor-fugitives with no place to go

Black swans and ash swans
Come gliding across rivers of deadly gold
To hear the singing of a map

Feathers quiver, shake off flame in time
Beat away the pain in time and out of time
Rain falls off sacral wings

And in an acorn boat, bobbing down a rivulet
Twin children lie, small as ladybugs
Wingless, naked, humming

You were born to die, the musician sighs
But not on this hard tide!

She set the bug-babes on swan's back
With warrior-mother mouse as protector
And silvereye, a wingless falcon, as guide

Here, she said, is a necklace of moon-wrack to cling to

When the shadow-roads sting you and fear bites hard

Also, songs to memorize...
Fugues of wind and sea
Las pinturas embrujados
The aleph bet and such
Bezhig, niizh, niswi, niiwin...

These are signs of being

She sent the troupe to Other-Far-Place
Their travel powered by groove, and time

On arrival, safe from slanders and other burnings
The wetlings and their friends found a lake of emerald ice
Preserving the last tale in its frozen arms
The last day, the last moment, the last song, and breath
All, held safe for later
Half-lives later

Taste this, the bow-woman said
Dipping honey-cake in waters of green thought
You two are not to blame, so small and ignorant

Sleep now, 'til you grow past acorn pip
Learn to think a bit and turn the rocks for deeper looks
Stop your shouting and your fights
Listen good

Do not return to flame and wood
Calling your nameless names again
Not 'til you hear me play the sun
Then you'll know that I've won

(Though my dreams smolder in blistered palms
And I own nothing but a horsehair bow)

Come home!

Music makes a pattern—find
Up-stitch, river-braid
Rhythm caressing rhyme

Playing sunbeams, plucking cloud
What's undone will be remade
My ugly doves
What was lost, recalled, regained
A home made of this homeless home
This placeless place

An exile's stubborn grace

Know, children
Hear what I say

Many hold no love for you
Some may even come for you
My songs will always ring for you
Listen for the sounds of light!

Here is my gift and legacy
This amulet of imagery
Keep it in the sky of you
Deep inside the earth of you

Become your own wee ancestor
Your bitsy monster-guardian

Spin your beats and songs
Your rants and rhymes
From all life lays in hand and mind

Bespeak your fierce and gentle path
You will survive!

LIMINAL ROUND

1

Wild midnight punches her card late
Mosquitoes attack with pitchforks
Woodpeckers emerge from the underworld
To scour the hemlocks
For subversive sentences

2

An unrisen sun rages
Sucks shadow-bones
(No dawn soul)

True night opens wide her palms
Revealing an ancient pain, a weirder refrain
Sings

Come to me, fair-weather friend
We'll dance
Defying death, that killjoy

Bright stars laugh at celestial subterfuge
Celebrating their own, mortal physics

3

See how blue dawn hovers, still 'sleep
Between bursting fires and gouts of rain

Morning-person crickets are *hong cha* companions

A dump truck rattles my windows
Montez the columnist, is up and gone
Also, Miss Lu the lunch lady, who jogs

The Pleiades arrive late to the party

In a swirling splendour of lights

Ghosts from antique stories
Comets without bones or a future
No longer dancing perfect time

Like us

Singing on as mere echoes do
Rushing to pay the past-due bills
Scribbling hopeful to-do lists

Reviewing and renewing
Our phantasmagorical mathematics

Lucky I feel, don't you?
To witness the cockeyed shimmering
Sketches from an eternal messaging system

And my love burning dark within
I miss you so

4

I took silence for a walk
Nice day, I said

Hmmm, silence said
As if I'd interrupted some private thought

The sun rants on, even in calamity, I said
Spreads molten wings and laughs, laughs!

Silence smiled

Merciless you are, I thought
Like winter sun

(I didn't say it)

My silence picked a snowdrop
Wore me like a sleezy new dress

Constellations rained down in daylight, scarring my palms
That burns, I purred
No thanks to you, silence

Impatient with one-way conversations
I skipped, jigged, and blathered stupid jokes 'til silence broke
Ice on a sudden lake

Sky ripped away her gag
Shedding the weak tears of a day-moon

Silence can wear its own rags from now on
Howl at the insult in storm-words

I'll cavort with creation 'til twilight arises
Taking finite rests, only
Between extended choruses
Mere seconds of silence
(Mixed with drops of startled rain
and purple wine)

I'd drink silence if I could, not drown in it

Defy death, numbness
Sing to nobody
To all the caverns inside any self

This silence, finally my own

Reverent

5

What can I say but thanks, willow
Queen of the Roadside

Spring came without seed pods or leaf songs
Your bark cracked and peeled away
Nothing green caressed you
And even the flies fled

Once, your arms changed the weather
Now they await a last invitation
Join the invisible waltz

At dawn, a host of cardinals
Make a palace, elegiacal
On the wreck of your body

Weaving sun songs
To the tune of the real you
Your vast timeless root
That keeps singing

Inside the heart of the world

6

We chase evening shadows
Looking for signs of a singed heart
Hidden in the tangled brush
Of our mourning

We must find and pluck it
Before the clock strikes 12

Ah the reckonings!

Such beauty in the struggle with friend death

Who arrives in drought or bloom
In the middle of the cooking or the washing-up

And the lists of tasks, thousands of years long

Keeping us on our toes, ever in the throes
Weaving luminous webs
Of our shredded, ever-budding hopes

Reminding us of the extinguished fires

Those eyes
Milked, blurred

The loves that were

While we compose tender goodbyes
In advance

To every little, tiny thing
That is

Was

Or will
Be

WHOA DEATH

What shall I say to you, Death
In this time of all times

That you carved the bone of my breath
To a thin hard edge

That you mapped us with routes to shadow-waters
Haunted us with songs that can't be sung

That your raw tides marked our skin and all within
Scarring the earth of me and mine

Now, rendered mute with grief
Your subtle, bitter gift
We open our hands to receive rain
Are shocked by strange flows of joy

Scoured by pain flowing in dark rivulets
We become more beautiful

Learning
All that terrifies us
We will become

In the ultimate justice of night

And the result of your sacred equations, Oh death
Written in a calligraphy of winds and seas

Is that Love, Oh Death
Will be ours, always

Rooted deep as gold mountains

Now

And then

ANIMATE

Small hours crawl
Work of the heart, split on night's anvil
Sleepless, she wanders
Where the scent of fir is a caress
Even here on this explosive boulevard
Air is redolent with rain-thought
Dark breezes bring gifts of urban pollen
Puddles on heaving sidewalks flood sneakers
Burn chilblains
Her head is rearranged by memory
While slips of early day-shine rattle water-skins
Thousands of suns all down the street, look up
She steps over them
Mercurial messages from above
Manifest below
Reminding her what those wise heads taught
In voices disinterested
Without accusation
Way back when, and she was lost
Without roof or leaf
Or food for the coming week
Stepping across a stranger's fire
To find home

Hey, kid, they called

Feeding heat with birchbark burning best
Sucking hand-rolled cigarettes
Joshing the way they did

Don't step over flame like that
Nah, don't step across a fire
All busy, scars in your eyes
Planting numb feet

Without vote or mind
Searching for crumbs or bones
Forgot a pencil
To map your scribbles of inner flame

And you, eating time
Going hungry

Show some respect, fire-made

They said
Those ones now passed
Saving the world in an hour
With droll lectures, grief-deep

Don't go hurting things

Stomping the little or vast things of life
Not unless you're so damn good

You can fix them
And put 'em back exactly right

i hear those voices still
Animate, fiery
As the sun singes my days
Signing all my steps
Offering a gift
Of common, holy destruction

Well-taught
i give thanks

Always

NAPALM HEAD

Papers are splayed in black and white on linoleum. Da slams
down the cup, coffee spilling over newsprint. "Poison. Damn"
Peeking over his shoulder I hear, *poison hand.* He shoves me
Back—pulls me close. A girl runs down a dirt road. Planes reel
overhead. Cameras snatch fire-seared fields, collapsing villages
A famous photo is made. Bare skin is draped in napalm. Da points
out the window at the blue universe, a bird diving. Our skin
drinks time, sky folded into story. Hers is doused in fire. Nobody
tells me her name, her name. Fleeing bombs bursting in air, she is
somebody. I'm somebody looking. We are dressed in poisoned
garments made in the U.S.A.   Napalm head, oh, wild thing

Midnights awake, dreaming ash-lands, I play cards beneath
thin covers. Hearts are diamonds, glittering under pressure
Spades make weapons. Clubs are riven clover, a burnt mouth
of fright. Da says we're apple pie, bomb 'n' lie. The girl runs
He curses. Pages are splayed wingless on a linoleum table. Relic in
monochrome. Her pictured cry pierces my membrane
In dreams I take her hand, say, what's your name, your name?
Bombs burst in air, relics of feeling, of unmeaning. America
manufactures strangers, infants of torn cloth. She ran down a dirt
road under fire. I heard news of war. It hasn't ended
Napalm head, oh wild thing

We go to a peace march. Women paint placards. "My man is
in the infantry, stationed around Da Nang," says one. "Heard
nothing from mine, 9 months," says another. Her voice is storm-
struck birds. A red afro is fire around her face. Fingers tremble
and she paints her sign in bright-feather ache. "Bring George
Johnson home." A sigh. "Yeah sis, yeah." The ladies finish their
work, pat gleaming updos, adjust floating scarves before entering
the street, nameless. *Bring my man back home!* Gazing up
at the red-haired lady, I feel universes throbbing under

freckled skin. Rent, bills, and the kids. Her mama helping out, but
faltering. Husband at war, far away. Yet she smells his head on
the sheets and the dead, midnights. Charred clover, riven sky
Oh wild thing

I decide to make a placard too and choose my colors. "Bring my
husband home." I sign my name with blue of diving birds
The ladies giggle into work-chapped fists. I am funny
I've become everybody, a relic of many persons, a riven earth
Trauma solitaire. Oh, wild thing

We march at the protest. Men in suits and baseball caps laugh
with menace. "Hippie-lefty mob blocking traffic. Shoot 'em up, ha
ha." Kids made symbols, strangers, targets. Riven sky, diamond
heart. Torn membranes, apart, apart. I hurry across the street. My
protest-sign stabs airless air, a relic of feeling. My husband is
missing, my child, dying. Skies burn, peel, and crack

Night-sticks ready, police charge. Crowds tumble through tear
gas, shouting. Hearts, spades, clubs, diamonds—like herded
together with like. Somebody throws a rock. It splits my mouth
I still have the mark, an emblem of unmeaning. Guns pop! Sirens
beat and bruised bodies fall. Shamed, I think, I got no husband...
ABC, 1,2,3. Stupid kid, learn your colors. Oh wild thing

7 split crows spill across chapped, shredded sky. Mind ripped from
mind. Apart, apart. In lands of unmeaning, wars happen
elsewhere. Border rez, rice steppe, fields of stoop labor, a
metropolis of kora-playing scholars. With poison hands, we make
strangers. Not one with mourning feathers or refugee
rivers.

I was instructed so, a fresh dismember of the indoctrination. One
hallucination under a slandered god of explosive gases. False
membranes attached with barbed wire stitches. Trauma solitaire
in black and white. Oh, wild thing

And the charred village. The ash harvest. Infants of torn cloth
Children bombed, shot from sea to shining sea as a part
of doing business. Flaming palms, leaves flailing, weeping silence
as trees do. Men shoot men point blank. The head snaps back
Crack! Crack! Crack! Papers are splayed across linoleum. Oh, wild
thing! Children run and run. Da curses. A million years of
ancestral invention gush backwards. Pop! Pop! Pop!
Napalm head apart, apart

And the burning monks fold gently into dark earth, robes
ignited, floating. And their prayers dance on flames. And our war
spills out a black and white T.V. News at dinnertime, laden forks
suspended in trembling fingers. And the child GIs, also
monochrome, expire on agony stretchers, weeping on film for
their mothers. Napalm head, oh wild thing

Years and years later, the girl from a famous photo rises off
splayed pages, emerging from black and white, speaking and
telling. *Kim Phuc Phan Thi* says her name again, again, again.
Narrating her road, telling her way

Me, I tear at poison garments made in the U.S.A., finding another
layer, and another, shredding skies as they unspool
leaving a burnt mouth of fright

Somehow, Our country doesn't learn shit

Oh, sing a song of the peaceful bullock, the ash village. A riven
night splayed across linoleum in black and white. Stars that turn
away, mourning the wounded dark. Monochrome camps
in empire, making strangers on dusty roads. Harming the small
as a part of doing business. Torn membranes stapled, wingless
A scent of the dead at midnight, protesting

Sorrowful, sorrowful

the marching women

the weeping
                    trees

        Refugee rivers crying out

                for memory

            Children fleeing, running, running

                Now, feel
                    riven clover

    minds ripped from minds

                        hearts from hearts, apart

    apart

                And the shards of history

                    of unfeeling
                        and unmeaning slicing
                            up our mouths

        Napalm head

            Oh, wild thing

                    Remember

    Speak

FUGUES & FRACTALS

2 Pi R

I.

I'm fond of my local café!
They serve all kinds of pie
Selling out by noon

If you get there early on Saturday
You can have peach, blueberry, or savory

I imagine fat peaches sweating among kidneys on a cutting board
I wonder if they communicate one with the other
About war or livid transmutations

The chef wears heels that click across the floor, meaning no harm
I enjoy the sound of heels on tile, so clean and crisp
As if this world of chaos was well in hand

Right here at the café

The tiles are black and cherry red
They gleam after their morning soaping
Hinting at friendship
Enhancing an illusion of peace and comfort

Welcoming also are the round tables
Scratched and rusted
Even the cast-iron chairs
They do not bite or snitch

A sturdy coffee cup soothes my unease for half an hour
There is much to thank coffee for
Yes, I've walked through time and trouble
To another natal day

I always spend birthday afternoons in a café

Such places, sanctuaries
Frequented by artists through the ages
Make me believe anything is possible
Or at least something

Today at Pie Time café
Millions of people fight thousands of wars
Families toil in petroleum fields
Revival tents sprout from the crusts of earth
Riots occur and bulldozers demolish a town
Last butterflies migrate, using cloud signals to navigate
Forests flourish then wither under tables laden with tarts
Moody seas rage and howl, tossing cups and saucers skyward

Folks pray, laugh, lie, sip tea, spill secrets
Pots bubble and heave
Cutlery clinks, discussing topics of interest
To bent forks, dull knives, and stolen spoons

Life and history are here
In each breath and sip, like it or not!

I listen with devotion to the symphony
Voice on voice, rolling, clamoring

Cold milk pours from pitcher to cup
Emitting a sound like no other, nearly Niagara

Pure waters tumble from a great height
On top of themselves

Originating at a glacier older than consciousness
Kissing limestone farewell as it disappears

The air has grown yeasty

Cinnamon, hot peach, and honey reign over me

Such scents recall fall, lurking snow
Toothy snares crouched, whispering in birch groves
Fresh-killed meat on pure white bone

And again, the tiles, crimson and black, I admire
Cut so neatly, laid skillfully
Embodying a flat aspect

Hinting at vast galactic spaces
Innumerable light-bodies slow-dancing

Now, consider once more the cup in my hand
A direct descendent of the first cup of all time
Thrown on a potter's wheel
Invented by a brilliant child—
Some budding singer, blacksmith, farmer
Seeking escape from another conflagration

A million years before this exact moment

2.
Once upon a time, I met a fellow outside Avora, Colorado
It was a café like this one, at roadside
Again, a birthday (not a million years ago)

Forest fires raged nearby and smoke burdened the wind
Elk leapt across the highway

We sipped coffee at the counter, his black, mine with milk
"What're you writing, the great American novel?" He asked

"A thing about a café," I mumbled, slamming my journal shut

"Gonna put me in it?"

"I could. What'll I say?"

"Say you met a good-lookin' guy
A long-distance trucker, pay in hand, headed home
First time in months, a weekend with the family
He was tired of living like this
Alone and always on the road

Taking a cig break in a Nebraska cornfield
He decided to throw in the towel
Search for work 'round home
Slim pickings sometimes—except the damn oil

But why not try? Our son coulda died
Ten-car pile-up in that wild spring blizzard
The kid came out alright in the end. Cousins, too
Sure clears a mind"

"Got a book of your own, sounds like"

"Hundred-fifty more miles to my door!
My woman'll kill me for quitting..."

"Mighty long drive through fire," I ventured

"Do it all the time!" He snorted, signaling to the waitress
"Slice of apple to go, sweetheart"

"Who set the trees ablaze this go-round, I wonder?"
She said, gazing out the window, a face like evening sun

"Make that two slices," he said. "2 pies r, ha ha"

"Unless you're short of pi," says I, joining the funny

"Back home, we share the pies." He winked at the waitress

She flipped long hair behind—three shades of onyx
"Want nothin' off you, bud." Brandishing a knife
She slid pie from the glass case
Cut slices, and placed portions in a white box
Lush foothills of brown crust collapsed into valleys of apple
The box entered a brown bag

(I like watching the doings of food, as my soul is ever hungry)

"Listen," he said. "Write this. *He was a Ute without the pie*"

"Want some?" I offered my quivery lemon meringue

"Geez, it's just a silly joke" He gulped the last of his coffee
"Ute, without the pie. So, not Paiute. *Ute*
Keeping it real simple for you
Get it right for once, okay?"

Ute, I wrote, stomach churning. Get. It. Right.

He slid off his stool, tossing bills on the counter.
"Actually we're Nuche. Our word. Say it, eh?"

"Nuche."

He shrugged. "Not too bad, I guess"

You know when you've misjudged something
Say, your own humanity
And by extension, everybody else's?
And your stomach knows?

You wake to find
The world is days, weeks, centuries ahead of you
Wide-eyed, electric with life, tapping a foot

Wondering (when it gets a moment)
If you'll ever rise up, wash down, and join the story

All the music stirring in the ground

You're a semi-provincial type, off-white, say, alienated
But your guts are insightful and *perceive things*
Like how all the beings are connected
Despite many crimes

That's why your culture is always trying to mangle them
Your guts
And your connections

With a loud pop!
A historical fissure opened beside my coffee cup
Before I could stop it, my pen slid away from me
Rolling into that steaming crack in space-time

Last, a fiery red rock crashed on the counter
Rattling dishes, east and west

Mr. 2 pies r was unbothered
He nodded to the waitress, grabbing the to-go bag
"I'll leave you to it. Be lookin' out for your book
Expect to see my face on the cover. Hey, I discovered you!"

I waved at the window
A heart-stopping view of mountains floated in tendrils of smoke
"I s'pose you belong to all that, huh?"

"Oh, you don't?"

I cringed. "How can 2 pi r work if all the circles are busted?"

"My circles aren't busted. Well, if some are, we'll fix 'em
I hope." He shoved through the glass door

"Mine neither." The waitress-artist sketched a burnt forest
Her pen flew across the little pad
A deft and practiced hand, she had. "Not busted"

Unbroken, I thought
May the circle be unbroken
Not busted

Plump, balding, shadow of a ponytail twirling
Defying time in a broad-shouldered way
Mr. 2 pies r mounted his big rig. Lit a cig
And roared out of the parking lot
Heading for his future, the son and fierce wife

All he belonged to

I don't think he caused the historical fissure that ate my pen
No, the flying rock came for me alone

History does flit about among happenstance
A wraith playing hide-and-seek at cafés
It will reveal you for a tool or a fool
Steal your implements or your tongue, bash your head in

You may miss moments of significance
Or accord significance to moments that have none
(Yet, is it fair to say that a moment lacks significance?
'Cause what might the moment itself think?)

Humility is called for

I imagined milk flowing backwards
Out of my coffee cup into a pitcher
From the pitcher to the milk can
From the milk can to the cow, etc., etc.

Cooked apples leapt out of a pie
Regained their crisp nature
Joined one another as whole fruits
Fleeing humanity

Seeking their *One Tree* at the beginning of all time

Hey, what if Niagara went backwards
Falling upwards into the sky?
What if stars were once water (or milk)
And that's why they cry?
What if the lies we told could be unsaid?
What if all the stuff we wrecked could be remade?

Still, the unravelings continue
No matter what I say

So I keep on trying

3.
Today, on my current birthday
I order another cup of Joe, sip
A clock ticks
I await the cousins (They're always late)

Meanwhile, milk flows from pitchers into cups
Not the other way, unfortunately

Outside the picture window
On which *Pie Time Café* is painted in blue swirls
Billowing clouds change shape in a rush
According to their nature

Within, I hurt

Weighted by memories that find no expression
It occurs to me that I wanted to write with a fiery pen
Change the world—or at least my town
I wanted to heave words like flaming rocks at our wrongs

I won't give up, though my tears produce little heat
And all is failure, amidst writhing tendrils of smoke

(I curse words, poems, my messy journal
Which cringes in pain at my violence
And dire lack of confidence)

The chair beneath squeaks
Begging me to shift the heft of such negative thoughts
Responding with a moan, the table asserts itself
No doubt having concerns of its own

The clock stops
Spirits swarm in and out of everything, everywhere
Saying, "hey, you up yet?

The Arctic burns

I think, wait, wait!
What of my scrawl
Wandering so far in search of a road, a pie
A circle unbroken?

The coffee cup extends itself
Clay parts, smooth and gentle
Offering that infinitesimal measure of love and agency
Belonging solely to coffee cups

The blessed vessel speaks
"I feel you, really, I do..."

POCKETFUL OF FRACTALS

Brilliant hues flicker, trapped
Spinning extruded gyrations
Flowering formations burst
Kaleidoscope days go upended

We live them

Children race circles in a barren yard
Dust flies, becomes whirlwind tapestry
Announcing the dead
And butterflies to come

Mayflies swarm
Flailing honey droplets from willow years
While night-things mark invisible territories
And lies are told as gospel

Church-bells ring dusk like it's 1492
And soon come a flogging or a burning
Police beat their sirens
Speed to dramas invented or otherwise

If nothing is shaking
Something will surely be shook
Tremors are felt in a parallel knowing
Us kids are warned not to notice

Or tell

Once upon a time...
We played London Bridge, toy soldiers
Sang ring-songs of small-pox seasons
Colonial unravelings
Drew in the dirt and invented our dances

While submerged histories
The crimes of ancestors
Jingle-jangled on the breeze, staining us

With bruises of a future healing
(Until you-know-who claimed us
I won't speak their names.)

Now, sizing up our many deaths
Athena's owl poses funny questions
Who is the mark, she asks, or the salesman?

Who is the bean counter
Of our irrelevance and weeping?

Who, the seller of empty words
A gutted dreaming?

Who killed memory
And for which mystery play?

Which yarn is vaunted again and again?

Whoooooo is the Curator at The Gate
To a palace of unmeaning?

Have we misplaced the apple
Of our invention?
Discarded the hopscotch of our rebellion?

Ashes, ashes, we all fall down!
(Not telling, not telling)

And where do they fly off to—

All the dead angels of agency?

LULLABY
(FOR GRACE)

soon will come a comet
new around these parts
to bargain with sun, whisper by Venus
we can't understand such laments
treaties between entities of the cold black
we take comfort in their balancing act
baby, rock the cradle, way up high
fly don't fall, not yet
through dreams
into the furrows of earth
and the next day, come
the crow who talks
and the goggle-eyed possum of the yard
and then, a rainbow
crossing the road
the moon wrapped in snow
shedding face
and yellow leaves tumbling
from red mid-winter thaw
the call of the white-tipped owl
in our sleep
the ache in us
when dawn flips beauty
her divining sticks
a long cry of violet waves
even if it is only in our minds
sea's harp
river-guests dancing sideways
on land dry as ancient dynasties
lost alphabets
wrapped in wine-soaked linen
a sip of ash

a dash of chamomile
frozen in amber
then, the brush of a wing
of another kind
offering brambles of word
sung
the ticking of a clock
under paper skin
measuring seasons
in hemlock rings and fir perfumes
the resin of wood years
and fractured light pours in, out
pitchers of honey
the milk of a goat
who also talks
summer rain
and the dry ochre wind
More days
of which we lose count
as if we held a bounty
to sift and spread
on slices of bread
of doubt
bread of sorrow
layers of bone
laced with sugar
wrapped in silver cones
hoping to be remembered
in the rust-gold dirt of drought
corn's mouth, the weeds
the raking of the days—
their seeds and calculations
now, touch the hours
and the nights
with our palms

placing hands on piano keys
a fingerboard
looking for a song-moon
duet with abandoned coyote
outlaw swan
a riff off veins of limestone
and bedrock
a secret face in the cliff
yawning
waiting long
longer
yes, we plummet
when we must
to meet earth's music
sung-up, singing
kicking
jigging
dressed in red cloth
black ink
silver beads
and other dreams

these things
these things

ALCHEMY

I conjured a name
For a leaf
Never yet seen

Also, an ache
Making me prey, brute
Unthinking

How real, they became
The named
How heady

Safe-cracking the shell
Of my flimsy oneness

Demanding a lexicon
For severed story
And unmoored stars

*

Distance bloomed inside
A sere prairie wind

The mind, regarding leaves
Bereft of trees

Halved
Seeds, stumbling
Flying

The spirit
Learning

New winters

FIVE SPIRITS IN MY MOUTH

1. Particle

Beneath dim sky
Neither noon nor dusk
At the entrance to a vast capital structure
Built of unwilling stone
I took a child in hand
 She'd been longtime lost
   Her forehead was smudged with fire
    I could help I thought, if I tried

   No time passed before more small ones came crowding
     Sudden as shrapnel
       Three, four, six, nine, thirteen
         Racing from behind massive pillars
          (Carved by artists indentured to demagogues)
           The wood splintered and the hinges popped
            Chirping tongues scraped the walls, crying out
             Slid down pipes, bashed the windows
              Demanding attention, truth, retribution

              The weak gave way
              The larger, thrashed
                The floor groaned and buckled
               From the weight of so many
              I bundled them in, a fragile rabble
             Though my lap was a small country
            (Over-confident of its goodness)

         Where am I? I wondered
             (My veneer of unknowing under full assault)
              What planet is this?
           What land?
       Wasn't I a fountain, centering the world?

Giving much, living to tell the tale?

    I realized with alarm
        One of these nippers
            Could be the next great physicist
                Or a talented baker of madeleines
            A bicycle mechanic
                  Saving rusted three-speeds from oblivion
            A singer, calling rivers

Sure, there's a meticulous, loony poet in this throng
    A Grass Dancer-rocket-scientist or four
        Some clever sewing whiz, bird watcher, pot-washer
            An herbalist, a boat builder
                Or a runaway on the railroad tracks, slow-dying
                  Frozen in that gesture of longing
                    Begging a fix to stop the pain
                Seeking answers from the cold, cold ground

Tell me now
    What can I do?
      Here they all are, under, on top
        Stacked to the ceiling
      Hanging from the rafters, ready to drop

        I don't have enough food in the larder
           Of my megalomania
               The cornfields of my exceptionalism are stripped
                My holy bump has shrunk in the laundry
            Of my indifference

        (The largess I offered was not mine to give, I see)
      Though my declarations of love traveled a thousand miles

    Snaring loss and buried truths
And hungers so old they can't be sated

Not with empty postures
Or promises rescinded

And now, itchy needs come barging in
Demanding a reckoning
(Also, problems so simple,
They could be mended with thread and needle)

Truth be told, I know a cold night on the library steps
On my knees, in my bones
The bite of no work and the shame of no plate
Truth is, not one creature exists
I can say no to

I must find a way
"Out of this alien place"
It may be a song
I don't remember which
I'm well past singing

Counting the seconds
before a coming explosion
I can't spot the edge of the clamoring crowd
Tears mount, mine, yours
Falling in buckets, tidal
Showing how we may be related
Our cells, our salts, our fevers, and rare earths
We, the trampled
The half-standing

Soon, the lake of sorrow floods, drowning all and sundry
History is made orphan
History herself, the lake
Weeping the water that is us
Shedding the light that is us
Or was

And they keep
Coming
The young ones
Swept away
On tidal waves of distractionaries
Breaking up on cliffs of denializms

2. Wave

Ah, these times
When a trillion stories pour into our heads at once
Ah, such days, when hope resembles complicity
When love words come too easily
When, eating, we take food from other's mouths
Learning how we're ants
Shoving specks of dirt from place to place
Still, even in this malaise, maze
Dreams arrive, stubbornly singing
And creativity
That deranged, beneficent spirit
Occupies the five spirits of our mouths
Forcing questions, histories like hallucinations
Dropping visions, lost-and-found puzzle-pieces
Art comes falling off our palms, sweet and bitter, wild
An inner rain, watering broken centuries

3. String, Thread

I ask
Is there a sanctuary to be built or remade?
Where life herveryself, is not compromised
By every breath we take
The histories we ignore

And can never shake?

Is there a wee house, undivided
  Where I might keep some souls safe for a while?

  Consider proximate/infinite, says a ladybug
    Says the sky
      Yes, I reply, taking metaphor-knife to hand
        Halving a self that is no self,
          (Only a sea of eternal cells and dark stars)

        Yes, I say, cracking the ribs
          Of discredited heritage
            Emptying sacks of stolen songs
              To make more space
                Opening the doors of a third lung—
              Scarred and black
                Also, the echo chamber
                  Of my prairie heart
                    Seeking transformation
                  Not absolution
                Or two-second-and-stir reconciliation
                  Not more phony gestures
                    Trussed up as solemn treaties
                  (immediately betrayed)

          Instead, enter, be warm
            We'll manage, like a nested doll
              Hidden, one within the other
                (Each demanding a voice)
            We'll reenter the universe
          A photon among many
        In our cloud of improbability
      Appearing, disappearing)

(Oh, particle, wave
    Wave, and particle)

        We'll become the layered onion of time
            A patchwork rag
                Egg of universes
                    Zygote of primordial symphonies

                This song of we, long forgotten
                Disguised by anonymous hands
            Dropped into a cracked amphora
        Shaped like a violated woman
    Stored in a cavern
        Miles below consciousness
            Under democracy's rubble

                Remember how I lived, the jar sighs
                    Don't forget my children, who are yours
                    Yours, who are mine

    Remember how I endured, murmurs the parchment
        Remember the loop of calligraphy and of yarn, telling
        Your breath, breathing itself

                Remember the birth inside the ending
                A gaping hole in the heart of being
                The end of you, the end of me
                A fragile beginning—

                Reconstituted narratives of multiple universes
                    In tongues restored and silences reversed
                        Giving breath and breadth
                    To smothered tales
                Of children ripped from the arms of love
            Of roots searching dark wounds for purchase
        And too, of debts paid

Reparations made

    A retreat from lands torn
      Off the hands of grandmothers

      Inside this flesh-seed of ours, spinning nowhere

        Before the quenching of the day
          I ask the world to permit my reentry
          I beg life to give me a last try

        Entreat humanity (In some better time)
          To remember mine

            Hey, kids, won't you throw me a sign?

            Cause look how the moon rises
                    And arises

                    Spinning and
        reeling...

Ah
Just keening

LOVE, FUNCTION
(FOR ANDREA)

I

think in patterns

$f(x)=i\pi\sqrt{ey}$ and other silly math
something luminous
seen through your window
of space-time belief

say, a mystery storm, or planet of grief

snowflake-amoeba, butterfly-leaf, turtle-shell-eye
x could be starlight, and i could be me
we could make a new equation
never heard, felt, or seen

stories come to life, animate-dreams
embodied lightening
Hope braided in

And our telling, shaping fate
(impinged on, of course
by other's tall tales)

still, digging in, we stubbornly sing

numinal melodies, fractal beats
you become you, the youness of you

us together, skin-geometry
shape, mood, sound, groove—this pattern we've found

which found us

we keep drawing, figuring
till we leap to ground

becoming our own
brand-new-constellation-sky-sound

oh, how we sing
and how we're sung

yes, we're sung!
until, together, remade

we come beautiful-undone

2

inside a spirit
there are rivers, seas, and planets
in four limbs, sixteen messages
a bridge of tendons over fire

there is sky in the core of every bone

on this leaf
on this palm
directions for living

this is you
learning your own topography
your own constellation

a book old as the light bodies
that write themselves on dark

yeah, you know yourself

by taking other spirits for a walk

on the ground
beneath the sky of you

beside the seas and rivers
which sing on the rocks of you

along the streets
in the cities of you

forming the form and mind of you

this is being
us, entwined

one in the other
the other in the one

spirits knowing themselves
becoming

inside us, worlds

A SIMPLE SONG

SHAKES HER WORDS

I.

La, la, la, hey
Memories unfurl
A path across tangled sky
New moons, speak!

Hey, I heard they mentioned a talking owl
Rambled on about some stag with an emerald rack
Yeah, if you cut it down
You'd be richer than kings, free

They always told long, tall tales
About those Shakespeare acres
That plot of hers
Folks tried to grab, map, plunder, unmake

Our acres bleed copper
Shit gobs of gold
And if you tame 'em
Tears and trouble no more

We locals had forgotten our lore
How a plunder-fest backed by rifles and the rope
Turned one short day into a long, hard rain
Into angry dirt rising up out of itself

La, la, la, hey. Wind stirs memory, then flies home again

I'll talk while I can, and tell of her
The one who stunned us all
From sweaty courtrooms
To the wide stormy sky

Her with the acres they meant to defile

Yes, they took her lands, her inkless meadows
I mean the thugs in black tails with the well-drawn plans
For the mine, the wormhole, the fine hotel
And the advancement of man

What about the thrushes
Chickadees, eagles, beetles,
Ants, frogs, and children, she said
You haven't heard their testimony

The thugs laughed
I'll get to all that!

See, over the years, stories of her came fast and thick
We had fish-tales alright
You'd hear them off miners, janitors, baby-sitters
Hunters, seekers, and those wild-broad hikers from afar

Truer yarns yet, came from rememberers
Local poets, songsters, mechanics, junk dealers
Card-sharks, gardeners, barmaids, cooks
Waitresses, housecleaners, mothers, and aunties
Who could spin truth or lies, or both
Stitching gold threads across every sky

We the debased, lost, snookered, and landless
Spilled our secrets, tongues running a'loose

There were a lotta players back then
One of them was that talking catfish, a queen
Keeping watch at the headwaters along with princess trout
An alligator mapmaker, a philosopher tortoise, a snake
And an owl, (aforementioned—Athena's own, to be precise)
Who broke bread with humanity despite everything
Treating us with democracy and decorum.
Amazing, eh?

Wait, the befuddled investigators mumbled
Who was the one with the words?
What did she have to do with those acres waiting
To be used and abused (again)?

This question was repeated over and over for years
Creeping down the necks
Of copper-suckers and rare-earth muckers
Who shivered through feverish nights of digging, probing

To no result

See, the speculators who stalked that land
Ended up haunted
They'd bag a bear, or deer, or oil well
Hurry home
And find their booty had disappeared

They'd net a catfish
But the scaly thing would haunt their dreams
Night and day, years on
Showing up at the family barbecue
Sucking down the bourbon
Blabbing 'bout all your dirty deeds

Now, the well-fed, shiny hippies and anthropologists
Unearthed no clue
Making noise about orchids and daisies
That gave you new names, slant dreams

Even bowed to the mud, prayed

Those anthropologizers had a theory about the place
But declined to prove
As proofs in this case, geological, or digital
Could only serve as more rope

On which to hang the local spirits
Or bind and gag the throbbing hearts
Of the precious ore breathing below—so, they left
And never returned, for which many thanked them

The locals left behind, who had less fuel
Fewer degrees of possible separation
i.e., the kids, mechanics, teachers, singers, cashiers
Farmers, roofers, ditch-diggers, etc., etc., etc., and I also

Searched for the story of *her*, hoping to save the world!

In the end, we did as suggested
In a certain ancient book we found and passed around
(A yellowed almanac with a map scribbled on the flyleaf
I can't say more)

We packed a lunch and got up our courage
Ventured up Eagle Head to the mouth of the Antler
Where we lived when we were much poorer or richer
And followed the rhythms
Of seasons, waters, constellations

There, we'd find out (we thought)
Who had created this endangered largess
The supernatural fields, the talking fish
And the rebellious acres with a will of their own

Some of us indeed lusted for gold at the end of rainbows
Buried treasures, forever-paid bills
To ease our troubles
Since we were disinherited from the dirt

And the yoke of reasonable work

Some of us dreamed of other things
Things that aren't things

Say, star signs, sand tracks, melodies, primordial arts
A place or space of belonging

We dreamed of days
Without soporifics, conspiracies, or spirit-killers
We imagined chants in candle wax and leaf fall
Lost sounds, alphabets, raindrops, wolf-prints

Old wife's lore and hidden customs
Utterances that can take you down
Or lift you over
Into a life worth living

Yeah, a measure of hope

(Not all that marketeering and whatnot, though—
the perfect visages, ever-unscarred)
But some primordial algorithm or geological dance step
An elemental numbering system, song or way of being

Do you get me?

Anyway, to continue
We crossed the mossy bridge, barefoot
Found yet another rickety way spanning more rivers
More tributaries, more veins of the world

Lone we were
Mournful in the dark
Afraid of losing ourselves
Though we hadn't found ourselves yet

In the end, it was the way that lost us
Wound itself up—the road, I mean
Becoming a rag rug on which we slept

In the wee hours the ground heaved
As we snored
As we dreamt
(Something to do with its nature)

That rug rolled us up inside itself, I swear
Or maybe it was the road, gone rug-like
Transforming itself into a snake
With us encased within?

Yes, we became an integral part of the whole schlang
Which bit us from inside-out, while biting itself, also

And due to the poison elixir we'd sipped
We slept longer, too long indeed
Waking, we could no longer remember the route home
Or our own names

Consider
Were we meant to be scarred by a forked tongue—our own?
Were we meant to digest our own tail?
Were we meant to lose ourselves, generations on?
And so, find her?

After many mishaps and adventures and tests
We were indeed allowed inside!
(I can't describe the container)
We finally met the one we sought!

Shakes Her Words

She was floating at the edge of perception
In a time that was no time
A place that was no place
In a home that was no home

She and her voice simply appeared!

2.
I will tell of her now (She said I could)

If any being managed to accrue light, fire, and ash
It was she!

You had to watch your ears and mouth
Around Shakes Her Words
'Cause you'd find yourself at sea
With your habitual excuses and lies

Your subterfuge, denial, slaughtered histories
Euphemisms, ugly slanders, bad grammar
Straw men, exaggerations
Scapegoats, erasures, phony sighs

You couldn't pull any colonialist wool across her mind
Or convince her that she was invisible, unsuitable
Ugly, useless, too much this and that...
Oh no!

She kept her electro-chemical fields sharp and clear
Knew more about us than we of her

Nights, she took the shape of a black swan
You don't mess with swans, as they will do you in
When she wanted, she could be that catfish queen
Long as a canoe—or the owl, aforementioned

She paid court in the fields
Under the waters
In the sky and on the mountaintops
Don't ask me how

It was something to do with a certain black ore
Alive in her hand

(No display of compliant eye, hand, lip
Gold largess, copper honey, sweet diddle, or holy-moly wah)
But sharp, fierce sound
Word-arrows!

Oh, she drew metaphorical blood when pressed
Herding verbs, plowing rhyme
Respectful most times
Deadly when required

That's why the name—Shakes Her Words

The People exclaimed
Listen how that woman shakes her words!
She sure told 'em, eh?
She sure showed 'em!

She sure set 'em back on their heels!
Had those fools spinning in circles!

Yes, her mouth could make the sky fall
Send lightening fleeing for cover
Storytellers even left off the ends of their sentences
Shrugged, saying

Shakes Her Words...
Well, you know—that one!
She gets inside'a you
Turns your guts backwards and inside-out
With home truths and hell truths
She'll show your ugly ass to your own self!
Look out!

3.
So, there we were at last
In the place recently baptized
Shakespeare's Farm
Where the unimaginable walked

Now we knew how it got that name
Not off the Brit with the flowery wordage-tillage
But from her, that warrior-Gran in an apron:
Farmer, herbalist, potter, lawyer, blacksmith

With leathered feet, callused hands
Who fought for the dirt
With nothing whatsoever apparent
Only a voice

Mellifluous, brilliant
Stubborn, and haunted
Her mighty words morphed
Joining with the land

A land that proceeded to fight for itself

You could not build on those acres
You could not dig them up
You could not poke that ground
Or pluck it or eat its innards

You could neither map, nor track it
Not traffic, trade, sell, buy, or plan for it
Though you may try
All deluded, greedy, and mesmerized

Even the mud would laugh at you!
That land would up and fight you

Mess you around
Finish you, for true

I mean, the sinkholes, the earthquakes
The toppling trees and winter beasts
I'm talking, mind-reading mosquitoes, ass-chomping bats
Soul-sucking quicksand, and raging derechos

That acreage had a power, come from her tongue

Those words
Those verbs
And rhymes
Sha-sha-sha-shakin'!

This was how she earned that name of names

Shakes Her Words

Her meanings brought lightening
Her dreams bespoke themselves
Her catfish-swan-woman sound drew forth a motley family
Of disinherited persons

Anyone, lost, cheated, battered, bereaved, maimed
Disinherited, insulted, robbed, deceived, shamed
She invited them all in
Built a town and a society

Amongst willful fields and copses and groves

She kissed the ground like some holy serpent
Knighted humble seekers with her handmade broom
Scrubbed away our sorrows in a washbasin
Her hands inside the night

In the clouds
In the blood

She planted an apple tree
Whose shade she named
Library of Liberty
Little Hedge School

So we can sit together in the cool
Reading, writing, mapping stars, remembering
Thinking and singing together
Making stuff as the healing dew gathers

No matter what they do

The wind rattled the branches
The leaves, said *yes, yes, yes*
Her apples, pears, and cherries
Fell close to the tree

She never toppled, herself

This primordial lawyer, mayor, and queen
Who was also a blacksmith by the way, did I already say?
A friend to strange metals
That bloomed and curled for her, like petals

Though she grew tired, weary
Her feet hurt and her knuckles swelled...
She never left her people
Her place, her truth

Always made way for some soul
Needing a hearing or a heel of bread
She never gave in
Never capitulated

And as I tell it, I'm there again

One of her very own
'Cause I declare she never left me
Though I was born in another era
Had to travel many moon-miles to find her sound

I feared for so long
There'd be nothing to know in the forgotten dust
Under the trampled grasses of mystery and silence
In the kitchens of chapped hands

At the top of the hurt, severed mountain

On a land named for some man
Who'd never even been here
Who'd never, ever
Loved this dirt

No voice had I or honest mirror
So, I tried to imagine, feel, and hear her
Still, it may be that I failed her and myself
She was only a woman after all

Bleeding, grieving, yearning, fighting, hurting
She was made of flesh

And flesh cries

4.
They, the dirty bastards, the sheriff and his goons
Came at midnight with shackles and no warrant
Took her, creeping 'neath the cover of vile slanders
Since their act could not bear the scrutiny of day

Yeah, their overlords wanted that land of hers

And they were bought men

Folks tell
They shipped her east, though we were east itself
Or buried her deep in the western mountains
Though we who loved her were of the west-places
And surely would have seen

Or they dressed her in stones
And dropped her in the river

Which she then called home

No boulder or rock would turn a hand against her
No water agree to swallow her
It was a drought year, too!

Some say
The soldiers cut her wrists to disguise their work
Tied her to our apple tree-library
For ten starving, thirsting days
Set a fire at her feet

As if they must kill her three ways for death to take

The apples came night-red and salty, generations on

Except we would have felt such crimes, wouldn't we
In our bones and soul-boxes?

Gathered together beneath that dark shade
In our library of grief
Our library of tortured liberty
We would have tasted such flesh-fruit and known

Wouldn't we?

Those horror-tales had to be a lie
To make us give out!
Make us forget everything
Even ourselves and her—and finally, join the rout
Right?

5.
How it really happened:
Her gifted, just mouth was stuffed with raw cotton
Her strong arms of a blacksmith, potter, farmer
Were bound behind her

They sent her packing for speaking her mind
Dismissed her, cursed and threatened her
Witchified her, scapegoated her
For being strong-willed

They scrubbed her histories and her names
Her images, deeds, ways, claims
Ripped languages off her tongue
Sliced knowledge from her flesh

They stole from her, her body and its story
Plundered her vision, ideas, work, lands
Left her in shadow
Erased and unknown

They spiked her drink, so she'd lie down
A proper senseless doll
Laid her on a pool table
Had their way with her a thousand years on

They parted her legs, one from the other
Like a divided, plundered country
Or in a dark alley, at the office or the after-party
They stove in her face, broke her skull

Carved their names on her, laughed
Burnt her on a pyre
Cursing her to hell
Found so many ways to do her in...

Depending upon
Who she was, her history
Where she came from and when
Who she wished to be

We called it normal

Refused to hear her screams of protest
Or believe when she hollered
No!
Stop!
I'm in pain
Enraged
A person, exhausted
Scared and lonely
Bleeding
Dying

Oh, how our mouths hung open, catching flies

Yet, how could we be surprised
When the powerful, as ever, enjoyed impunity
While we muddled along, ashamed, complicit
Refusing to know

That we too were of them
And of her

While the foremother of our town, our world
Stood tall in that fleshly conflagration, weeping

How loved and cherished she was
We said, feeble-mouthed

Maybe we thought the words
And forgot to say them

We left our courage at the threshold of the world
We let the killers walk

Listen, great sun and moon on high
There were more of them!
They were stronger, meaner, louder
Richer, more famous!

They were armed
With a weight of law on them
They were decorated, shielded
Unhinged!

Besides, what of the children at home and hungry?
What of the crop to get in?
What of the taxes, the mortgage
The merciless landlord

What of our exhaustion?

Then too, what of the promotion?
The bribes and the kick-backs
That longed-for advantage?
The back-forty we'd cast an eye upon?

Yeah, our tongues stuck to the roofs of our mouths
Became homeless

Our language curdled
Our culture rotted

They took her while we watched

She didn't scream
Could only hum through that gag
Yet the foothills heaved
Rain crashed down
Thunder and lightning crawled 'cross the ground
Sobbing

Our soldiers stared into the sky
Almost dropped her
Fear swarmed their naked limbs like biting ants
Snapping at their bombast

The general put bayonets to bruised, flushed necks
Shrieking *Do it, dammit! Finish it!*
(That man was a berserker
And she was done for)

Meanwhile, a fair trial was loudly promised
By the blathering, sanctimonious
Priest-sycophant
Scuttling at the general's side

However, her wounded body was lost
On the way to the courthouse
We've seen such tricks before
Justice goes missing down the same alley daily

With extra, overnight postage and a hundred excuses

While apologies come quick and sincere
As a torch to your home and barn

Medicine-Field-Betwixt-Rivers
Our place, our home, our town

(They call it Coalville now, you know)
Was forthwith undone

It was for the trillions in copper and gold
The sky that shat money
The goose that laid be-jeweled eggs
The stag with an emerald rack

For coal and madness, broads and asses
Realizms and religion
The elemental world styled some boss-man's private bank
Toy-ranch-brothel-penthouse-gated-palace-empire

We'd be the stooges, the tools, the willing used
Playing monkey-see, monkey-do
We'd be the flag-waving spears for the nation
Killing her and ourselves

Well...

All the crops failed that year
And winter came too soon
The mine shafts, (built by the berserker's cuz)
Collapsed thrice

Overnight, the gaping holes
Blown in earth's bones were refilled
With pottery shards, rusted nails
And incriminating documents

Workmen fled
Afraid of ghosts, demons, indictments
The trees fell on them, sacrificing wood-selves
Swirling mud rose—not golden

Our rivers caused a revolution

While the wind ranted in every ear 'til we howled!

Those explorers with maps and plans
For the advancement of man
The soldiers, homesteaders, pioneers, thugs
Brought in to grab what could be snatched, blood-cheap

They all ran, ran, ran

But enough about them, though they are us

Listen, had she called on her earth—
And taught it to protest?
Or had the Earth instructed her
Lending a voice?

Not that woman = earth
But that we're all of dirt
Star, stone, moss, air
Water, dirt, worm, tree

In any case, she, Shakes Her Words, remains
If we listen
We learn this, in our bitter mouths
In our scarred hands and hearts
In our us

If we can recall that womankind is real at all

We fools, farmers, miners, shopkeepers, lawyers
Waitresses, janitors, musicians, librarians
Artists, cooks, builders, sweepers, teachers
Bankers, oilmen, big cheeses

Shrugging in our helpless malaise

Popping a night's sleep
Smoking something, punching something
To bury a nameless pain
To smother the cry buried within

While pounding another mountain down
To feed our mortal hides

Somehow, despite our vast, cavernous lack
She would not give up—
Neither on us nor on herself
She stalked our dreams, fighting our weakness

Shaking her words
Her words shaking us

Though why she bothered, I really don't know!
What was in it for her?

Maybe she was fighting for the souls of rivers
Waters and mountains and finches and fishes?
Maybe she was singing black ore to life
Maybe she was serving the stars and creation itself

The children, the future to come

Perhaps it was not about us at all-at all

Still, she whispered in our dreams
Demanded we recognize one another

She said
Stuff no soul in a character-warehouse
Never lose the five spirits of your mouth
Or the five thousand stars of your mind

Don't trash the five million seeds
Of a good dream
Or close your heart to the voices
Of those you've hurt

'Cause one fine morn the dirt of this land
Shall roll, rock, and rumble once more
Humankind shall take this shit no more
And everything will change

She murmured this in my ear one stormy afternoon
Or maybe that was me talking to myself...

Still, I swear, that Shakespeare tract
Brought her song back for real
Straight into the hearts of children
And out their singing mouths

Isn't it strange how her name was forgotten though?
Like she had to be some Shakespeare
To be remembered at all?

Anyway, we roused ourselves, bit by bit
Had to, though it itched, burned, and ached
Her words were water to a maimed and ruined tree
Sustenance for a starving heart

Even now she talks to all who hear
In the air, the star-rains, the thunder-jigs

See, she borrowed the voices of fishes, raptors
Horses, stones, trees, and roses

I was one
One of her many seeds

Her lost beads
One of her many tongues and songs
Traveling time

She was indeed a collector of seeds
Of growing things
Beads of meaning—
Her beautiful, powerful chain of being

And we were looped on her generous strands

Thus we remembered
What we could never have seen
How way back then—
After they made her drown, burn

Disappear

While our ancestors and we
(in this future-seeing)
Watched
Oh, just *bought*

Some brave ones ventured out

Scattered her necklace
The seeds, the beads flying every-which-way
Spreading remembrance like a claim
Sowing her words and hopes and dreams

Far and wide into a future

So that she, Mother of Words
Would not die

If here, not there

If north, never, ever to the south
If west, forget east

With many spirits howling in our mouths
We recalled her fight, her moods, her fires, and lights
How she overindulged, if possible, on apple pie
Rarely said no to a sip of berry wine

How her left knee offered no end of trouble
And oh, the swollen feet, the one bad eye
Her chest wheezing like an ol' accordion
When she cried

Amid that plain remembrance
The world moaned and shifted

The stag reappeared

Also, a giant golden bullfrog
A herd of poet-horses
A bat family, shrieking
A loon and a talking owl

Right after the scattering of the beads, see?
The scattering of her seeds
The discovery
Of hidden memory

Look! We hollered
The Queen catfish has come
Could that dark, luminous one be her
Her own self or her emissary?

People, listen! Some ragged dreamer hollered
Do you see how time and space have danced in circles?

The beginning has become the end
And the end is beginning all over again?

Who are we?
What is time?
What is death?
What is hope?

Will you join us, in our sorrow, our wrack, and ruin?
Letting lay the slander, mining claims, and plunder
The grabbing, grasping, smashing, taking, raping
The murder of hearts?

Life is a vine
Crawling on sweet, low earth
Fruiting out despite us
Blooming in silence

Becoming a green gourd, singing out
Which, laid to rest and ruminate in amber light
Transforms into an instrument of life
Of resistance

Of music and making

We've been such criminals, yeah?
Some more than others
Still, we can sing the stars back to light
My scarred country, my battered world

Even in this pain of ours
This torque of manufactured war
Mangled story, buried history
And hate

We are the songs

That life sings about itself

6.
I saw that stag with the emerald rack one time, I swear
Saw it leap into being
Born from one of her beads or heads
The ones we'd scattered

That stag went prancing, adorned in those strands
With a herd of elk friends and five coyotes
Bright colors were heaped around their necks
Seeds of meaning, jangling, dancing

A loon sang, too

We were changed

I even heard the west wind talk one time
Said, *I'm an old friend*
Born of a purple rock she cherished
And kept warm in her apron pocket

Bed-talk that wild wind made
Skin fever

That talking breeze blew seed-fuzz all over the fields
Flowers sprouted, nuzzling one another
Poems rained down, full of kisses
A black swan floated across a sky river

Singing honey

True gold was born
Light and a future
Memory came alive
I felt this, saw this, heard this

Always, ever, those lights
Her mud eyes, blue night, black sea
Appear to us
Strange stars in midnight's embrace

Her clever, scarred, eloquent hands
Cinnamon satin, turquoise silk
Turning the pages of an earthic book
Re-rooting the clouds to timeless dark

And love to all our works

We remember her now—all she was

Yes, I carry this fragile string of remembrance
Making my tattered scrap of life
Into a world
A whole universe!

My multiple voices are braided
Into one humming kernel
I wear an ark around my neck
A sign to those who know

Poems from a swan
Lectures out of a catfish
Songs off a rowdy singer
A womanish one

Her story, smudged, shredded, obscured
Keeps on living, shimmering

Yes, she kept her children thinking, rethinking
Analyzing, searching, telling, and asking
On this land that waits, bides it time
Under all kinds of cover

I'm not the only one, nor are you, believe me
Making, learning, doing, excavating, and remembering

The fields and waters
Also work
Throwing off their pain
They too, want to thrive again

Besides, we remember her now
Won't forget her again!

Roll on, stubborn tributaries, realign yourselves!
Let's sing for a blacksmith-lawyer woman!

A sculptor, painter, potter, builder, scientist
Mayor, farmer, mother, sister, fighter, granny
Librarian, thinker, wanderer, weaver
Herbalist, historian, card-sharp, auntie

Even if we don't know her face
Or her real name
We can say she was a teller of time
Of seasons and of Earth

She was a lover

Now that we've recalled her words and ways
Her places, days, deaths, friends, loved ones, and children
(While the ground under our feet cries, *fire, flood, danger!*)
Now that her image, her form, fill our emptied palms

Then what? She calls
What now, after a gutted dreaming?
What now, after all these wounded histories?
And the lake of sorrow over-flowing?

What are we gonna make?

7.
At twilight, tonight
Galaxies spoke
Through us
Their vast, cold questions

And Shakes Her Words
Sang once more
La, la, la, hey, memory unspools
From the mouth of the wounded dark!

Look how the fibers of the world come a'loose
Shadows walk, that are us
Violence walks, is us
Stories swirl in bent mists

Let her story come hot and clear
Words and melodies
Tongues remade
Deeds known

Our many debts, paid in full
'Cause each turn of the sky, we tell
Retell, make, remake, do
Our worlds be-speak

Re-speak, anew

Who do you plan to be? She shouts
Or her ghost, her spirit
Her path seeded with a million beads—also speaking
What will you do with a memory of me?

You, my children, old, and young

She says

What tales will you reveal?
What pain enshrine
Or soothe, undo?

What heart or bit of earth
Can you repair

And love
Love!
Just love?

Tell me
How shall we-all sing this life?

And

      How

           will

                  we

                          be

                                sung?

Gracias, 谢谢, merci, go raibh maith agaibh,
Danke, chi-miigwech, thanks

To the makers of forever & on who've formed me
I see your hands & hear your voices everywhere

To author/artist/editor, Emily Perkovich of Querencia Press
for saying the magic words & making a beautiful book design

You've been there since the first word hit the first page:
Andrea Hairston, Sheree Renée Thomas,
& in honor of the ones we lost:
Ama Patterson & Liz Roberts

To the art-friends/fellow travelers/family who shared their arts,
laughs, hopes, & insights with me, read my work, heard my
music, taught, & inspired me, or just hollered "keep creating!" My
moments with you have turned into story, song, poetry.
You're the light I live by.

Andrea Hairston, Sheree Renée Thomas, Eileen Gunn, Michel
Moushabek, Linda Addison, Danian, Darrell Jerry, &
James E., David E., Adele, Kevin, Roy, Sabine, Aoise, Camilo,
Sinéad, Ottilie, Rita, Bobby, Mary, Lily, Christal, Christopher,
William, Jada, Jackie, Grace, Nan, Han, Kiki, Fanfei, All the
Bavarians, Sasha, James T.W., Mei, Lino, Zola, Bill, Micala,
Glenn, John, Priscilla, La Tanya, Michelle, Tony S., David M.,
Paula, Ben, Greg, Sue, Sylvia, Jerry, Joy, Marcy, Myriam, D'Lena,
Olivia, Magdalena, Pearl, Bruce, Johanna,
all my students,
& the ones we always remember.

No art without love & trouble

ABOUT THE AUTHOR

Pan Morigan, a singer/composer/writer comes from the Great Lakes part of the world. There, the stormy sky is the landscape, the big story. Flat lands, with a long view, remind her to think through our current discord into history and beyond, to deep time. As a writer and musician, she re-finds her voice and purpose again and again in surreal times, needing speculative thought and the power of the embodied mind to conjure hope and resistance. Pan co-edited and contributed to *Trouble the Waters, Tales From the Deep Blue* for Third Man Books with Sheree Renée Thomas & Troy Wiggins, and has a story collection forthcoming with Querencia Press. She has written music for dozens of theater productions and performs her own music solo as well as with composer/instrumentalists Adele O'Dwyer and Steve Gores among others. Her music can be heard at panmorigan.com

*Photo by Robert Jonas

www.ingramcontent.com/pod-product-compliance
Lightning Source LLC
Chambersburg PA
CBHW071153120626
46546CB00006B/2240